A Life Worthwhile

The Story of Aaron

John Mollitt

Onwards and Upwards Publishers

3 Radfords Turf, Cranbrook, Exeter,
EX5 7DX, United Kingdom.
www.onwardsandupwards.org

This first edition published in the United Kingdom by Onwards and Upwards Publishers (2017).

ISBN:	978-1-78815-685-1
Typeface:	Sabon LT
Photography:	Photograph on opposite page courtesy of Simon Brown of *TravellingSimon.com*.
Graphic design:	LM Graphic Design

Printed in the United Kingdom.

John and Pat Mollitt, and Family

John was born in Lancashire, in the Lune Valley, and Pat in a Scottish coal mining village, in Lanarkshire. They met in Morecambe when John went to speak at the church Pat was attending. They married in 1972 and their children, Andrew and Joanna, were born in 1973 and 1976. Three years later, John was appointed pastor of Ingleton Evangelical Church and they became foster parents in 1985.

After two short-term fostering placements, Aaron came to John and Pat in November 1987 and was adopted by them in 2004. Until his death in 2016, Aaron was a much-loved member of the Mollitt family and treasured by many in Ingleton and the surrounding area.

Andrew is married to Sarah and, with his three children, lives in Singapore, whilst Joanna lives in West Yorkshire with her husband, Alan, and their two children. John and Pat still live in Ingleton, where John continues with an itinerant ministry and Pat keeps busy card-making and holding craft sessions for children in churches and community centres.

A Life Worthwhile

Contents

A Life Worthwhile

Foreword by Hilary Price

"It's a tragedy," the woman at the supermarket check-out declared.

"What is?" I asked.

"That boy being kept alive," she replied.

I looked to where she was looking and saw Aaron lying in his bed/wheelchair with his parents, Pat and John, at his side. The tragedy was not Aaron, but this woman's inability to see whom she was looking at, to see the wonder of Aaron, which is what John writes about in this beautiful book.

It took courage and compassion to foster and then adopt Aaron and to navigate all the ups and downs of life with a severely disabled child for twenty-eight years. John pulls no punches about the confusing, complicated and very frustrating world of Social Services, while at the same time showing how under pressure, a loving family can take on the world when they have unity, determination, compassion and a Christian life with boots on.

Aaron never spoke a word, but his life prompted a reaction in every person he met as the message he communicated through his smile was loud and clear: "I am alive and I matter."

As you read this book you will learn as much about yourself, through your responses, as you do about this extraordinary family. It took courage to live with Aaron; it took courage to write this book; it will take courage to read it and allow his life to impact you as it has impacted everyone who was privileged to meet Aaron.

Hilary Price
International speaker, Bible teacher, author

Hilary has been involved in the teaching of God's word for over thirty years. She is married to Charles Price, Senior Pastor of The People's Church in Canada, where, in addition to her responsibilities as a pastor's wife, she taught a weekly Bible study for nine years to over two hundred women. She continues to share her love for Christ and His love for her through teaching women at conferences all over the world!

A Life Worthwhile

CHAPTER ONE

Foster Parents

Pat and I always wanted children but we could not always agree on the number of children. We had two in the early 1980s – a boy and a girl – and I felt, on a pastor's stipend, that was probably sufficient. Pat, with her great love for babies and children, was not so sure and I knew she was anxious to have more. Pat's mother was one of thirteen children and, given the opportunity, I feared that Pat might try to emulate Granny Clark! Happily, we were able to settle on a compromise that suited us both.

We had stood as referees for a couple wishing to adopt children, and whilst being interviewed by the head of Lancaster Fostering and Adoption Services, Pat had introduced the subject of fostering. Nancy was a Christian and she, helpfully, gave us full information as to what fostering involved. Having thought and prayed about the matter, we eventually made an application, stipulating that we wished to foster babies and pre-school children. We did not want our own children – then aged twelve and nine – in any way to feel threatened, and we felt they could be fully involved in the care of babies and younger children.

Providentially, ten years earlier we had unexpectedly and un-officially had experience of fostering. 'R' was an alcoholic, and whilst in a psychiatric hospital he had entered into a relationship with 'S', the unmarried mother of three young children. One afternoon, 'S' asked Pat to look after the pre-school child and to pick the other two children up from school, as she was going to see 'R' in hospital. This Pat did, and the children had their evening meal with us whilst waiting for their mother to return. We waited and waited... but the mother did not come back, and when we made enquiries we found that 'S' herself had been admitted to the hospital as an inpatient.

We contacted Social Services, but as time was going on we had no alternative but to make beds for the children. Our hearts went out to them as they were now without a mother or a father. Initially, it was difficult for Social Services to contact the wider family and we were even asked if we would consider taking the children on a temporary basis. This we did not feel able to do, as Andrew was only four and Joanna not yet six months old. Eventually, the children stayed with us for ten days before arrangements were made for them to be cared for within their own family.

The process of becoming foster carers was, I am sure, far simpler then than it is now. We went to a meeting in Lancaster where, together with other prospective foster parents, we heard from experienced foster carers about the joys and challenges of fostering. We were then visited by a social worker called Peter who carried out an in-depth interview. I say 'in-depth', but when Peter discovered that I also was an ex-Morecambe Grammarian, much of our time was spent recalling teachers and pupils from our school days. Still, the interview must have gone reasonably well because shortly afterwards we were notified that we had been accepted as foster parents by Lancaster Social Services.

The wait for our 'first' child was not long and within weeks we were picking Christopher up from the Royal Lancaster Infirmary. His mother was an unmarried girl from Northern Ireland and she had been sent over to stay with an aunty, the intention being that she should have the baby and then give him over for adoption. Christopher was just six days old when, accompanied by Andrew and Joanna, Pat and I brought him home to Ingleton. This was the same hospital from which we had brought our own daughter home, ten years previously.

Christopher was a good baby but the first weekend was, to say the least, eventful. My brother and his wife had booked to go away, as it was their tenth wedding anniversary, and we had previously agreed to look after their three boys. So, in addition to Christopher, we had three other 'foster' children aged eight, six and four. We survived the weekend – albeit with little sleep – and so things could only get better.

Christopher's mother and great aunty came to Ingleton every two to three days and it was immediately obvious that mother was bonding with baby. Much to our delight, after five weeks, the mother decided she could not possibly give Christopher up for adoption and she was determined, whatever the consequences, to return to Ireland with him. Thankfully, her parents accepted the situation and Christopher soon captured their hearts. When he was ten years of age, Christopher and his mother visited us and it was a joy to see such a pleasant, well-mannered young man.

A few months passed by and then came a second call from Social Services. Michelle was a six-month-old girl whose unmarried mother felt she was not able to provide adequately for her. She had therefore taken the hard but courageous decision to offer the child for adoption. Michelle was an excellent eater but not a sleeper – something we had (or perhaps had not) grown accustomed to with Andrew when he was a baby!

Michelle stayed with us for five months and then she went to her adoptive parents. Adoption does not always turn out well, but this one has and twenty-nine years later we are still in touch with Alison (as she is now called) and her parents. Alison is now a mother herself and has brought her children to see us in Ingleton. It is most satisfying to feel that we perhaps played a small part in her early years.

CHAPTER TWO

Aaron Comes to Us

Eight months had passed by when I read in the paper that a four-week-old boy had been taken into hospital, having been battered by his father. I never said anything to Pat but I somehow knew that this baby boy would be our next foster child. So, it was no great surprise when shortly afterwards we were approached by Nancy, asking us to consider taking the child for a year.

Aaron was permanently damaged as a result of his injuries, and though not initially expected to live, he was making a recovery. Having had no previous experience of handicapped children, we needed time to pray and think about the possible implications. I remember being struck by the words of Jesus in Matthew 25:40 – "whatever you did for one of the least of these brothers and sisters of mine, you did for me" – and consequently we agreed to provide a home for Aaron.

It was a dull Thursday afternoon in November 1987 when we went to pick him up from the old Beaumont Hospital in Lancaster. This brought back memories because, in the 1950s, I had been admitted to the hospital with suspected scarlet fever. After three days, it transpired that I had German measles and there was no need for isolation and so my stay was a short one.

On entering the ward, we were met by a screaming child and a not too encouraging paediatrician. "I hope you know what you are taking on," she said. "He will never be able to thank you for anything you do."

I felt stressed as we waited for the paperwork to be completed; not because of the paediatrician or Aaron crying, but because I had someone coming to our home at 3pm to discuss their baptismal service.

It was an early introduction to what we were to learn many times over the years: be patient and always have a book or newspaper with you when you come for a hospital appointment!

"You have not destroyed him but you have destroyed any possibility of him ever having a normal life." These were the words of the judge as Aaron's father was sentenced to six years in prison. Both his parents had been heroin addicts and whilst nothing can ever excuse his action, there is no doubt that drug-taking was a significant factor in his father losing control.

Aaron was born with heroin in his system and this, together with his 'cerebral crying', made the first two months very difficult. Aaron literally cried for hours at a time and it was quite impossible to placate or to comfort him. We were sensitive to the effect this was having on our children but, in the providence of God, they both accepted Aaron into our home and immediately treated him as their brother.

We had weekly visits from social workers, and Nancy telephoned regularly to see how we were getting on. One morning, Pat explained that whilst things were challenging, we did have "divine support". Nancy laughed and said, "I know that is true but I cannot put that down on a Social Services report." Eventually Aaron settled down and life became more normal.

Aaron had many complex medical needs, and from the start much time was spent keeping hospital appointments. The situation was not helped by Ingleton's geographical location. Ingleton is in North Yorkshire, but our postal address is Lancashire and we are just four miles from the Cumbria border. This was complicated even further by the fact that though we were resident in North Yorkshire, we were fostering for Lancashire Social Services. Ludicrously, Pat took Aaron to three different hospitals in order to have his ears tested! We also discovered that 'professional jealousy' could creep in, even in the treatment of a multi-handicapped child. A medical worker from Harrogate, whom we greatly respected, had to stop visiting because Aaron was a "Lancashire child".

Aaron coming to us was a life-changing experience but we were determined that it would not impinge on the time we gave to the church. Pat took Aaron with her to afternoon meetings but it was not possible to take him to our Wednesday night children's meeting. One of our neighbours kindly babysat for us, but knowing how vulnerable and unpredictable Aaron was, Pat was never altogether comfortable with this arrangement. In the goodness of the Lord, our neighbour performed heroically and no harm befell either her or Aaron.

Sadly, not everyone was as helpful or encouraging, and there were those who thought we were foolish to foster a multi-handicapped child. "Don't keep him," and "Don't try to prolong his life," were two of the comments made to us. Pat and I can truly say we are grateful we never followed that advice, and though there were to be many challenging and testing times ahead, we never once regretted our decision. We mean it when we say that he gave us far more than we could ever have given him.

When Aaron was six months old, he smiled for the first time – and we felt elated. Having been given the impression that he would not be able to respond or communicate, this was something we had not been expecting. It was to be the first of a multitude of smiles to come, and for the next twenty-eight years it was his dominant characteristic. What we first enjoyed when he was six months old is what we miss the most today.

Another early memory of Aaron is that when I was taking a service, initially he could be rather noisy. We came to see that it was because he recognised my voice, and when I got into the pulpit, he thought I was talking to him. He responded by making sounds which meant nothing to others but which meant a great deal to us.

CHAPTER THREE

Aaron Goes to School

In bygone days, education for Aaron would not even have been a consideration, but this was the early 1990s and things had changed. Instead of being institutionalised, Aaron was entitled to a curriculum-centred education. He was classified as being a PMLD (Profound and Multiple Learning Difficulties) student and we began our search for a suitable school.

Again, our geographical situation was to cause difficulties because as our home was in North Yorkshire, the 'powers that be' indicated that Aaron must be educated at a North Yorkshire school. Consequently, an arrangement was made for us to visit Brooklands School in Skipton. This is an excellent school but it was for pupils with SLD (Severe Learning Difficulties) not for pupils with PMLD. There was not a wheelchair in sight, and when the head teacher asked, "Can Aaron walk?" we soon realised that, however excellent, Brooklands was not the school for him.

North Yorkshire County Council was, however, in a determined mood and tried to convince us that with additional staffing they could meet Aaron's needs. Around this time, we had a visit from Mrs Day, the head teacher of Bleasedale House Special School – a PMLD school in Silverdale, near Carnforth in Lancashire. Aaron's name had been given to her, and having spent an hour in her company, we knew that this school was the place for him.

We arranged to see Bleasedale House, and its educational, medical and recreational facilities confirmed all that Mrs Day had told us about the school. Mrs Day was a formidable lady and her parting words were, "Do not take no for an answer. Insist that Aaron comes to Bleasedale

House." Whether she was doing right by educational protocol, I am not sure, but she was certainly doing right by Aaron.

Thus, there began a struggle with NYCC which went on for several months. We asked the North Yorkshire educational psychologist to call and see Bleasedale House for himself. This he did and when we next saw him, his words were revealing. "If Aaron were my child, I would want him to go to Bleasedale House, but as the educational psychologist for North Yorkshire, that cannot be my recommendation." Not only was Bleasedale House the right school for Aaron, it was also eight miles nearer to Ingleton, but bureaucracy continued to dictate.

Pat and I were always eager to maintain our Christian testimony, but our patience was often tried by agencies which continually assured us that they were there to assist us but, at times, seemed to be working against us. Mrs Day and the North Yorkshire educational psychologist had both confirmed which school was the best for Aaron and so we were determined to 'fight' his corner. Proverbs 31:8 exhorts us to "speak up for those who cannot speak for themselves" and this we vowed to do for Aaron.

Eventually, I was asked to contact an educational officer in Northallerton who would make the final decision. Over a period of two weeks, I telephoned the gentleman in question eight times but he was never available. Promises were given that he would get back to me but he never did. On the last occasion – a Friday afternoon before the Christmas break – I explained that if Mr _____ was not prepared to get back to me, I had no alternative but to contact my MP. Miraculously, within fifteen minutes he was on the phone, apologising for not speaking to me sooner and, to my delight, confirming – if somewhat grudgingly – that Aaron could go to Bleasedale House.

It was a satisfactory outcome for us and, more importantly, for Aaron – but what about a single mother struggling to bring a disabled child up on her own? Would she have the energy or the know-how to challenge the authorities?

And so began, for Aaron, fourteen happy years at Bleasedale House.

CHAPTER FOUR

Hospitals and Medical Appointments

From the outset it was made plain to us just how severely handicapped Aaron was, and yet his disabilities were not obvious when he first came to us. After all, babies do not walk or speak or feed themselves and so, as a ten-week-old child, Aaron was very similar to other children.

Due to his injuries, he was diagnosed with spastic quadriplegia, epilepsy, severe scoliosis and severe visual impairment. Initially, these were just words and phrases to us but the implications were to become increasingly evident. And so, a lifetime of hospital and medical appointments began for Aaron.

In his pre-school years, Aaron had upper airway problems, with choking, snorting, gagging on his tongue and a dry mouth being the more noticeable symptoms. Consequently, he had an adenoidectomy and grommet surgery at Royal Lancaster Infirmary. These operations went well but did not prepare us for what was to happen later.

Aaron's right hip was dislocated and when the first operation was not a success, he was operated on a second time. After he was discharged from the hospital, we had one of our most distressing experiences. Aaron constantly cried, and for several nights Pat did not get to bed at all as she tried to console him. We called the doctor out, who could only suggest that it might be colic or that Aaron might have been traumatised by the operation.

After another sleepless night, we took matters into our own hands and drove down to the hospital and presented ourselves on the children's ward. Eventually, the surgeon who had performed the operation arrived on the ward – a man whose bedside manner left a lot to be desired. He was abrupt, unsympathetic and gave the impression that we were making a fuss over nothing. However, our social worker and the nursing staff shared our concerns, and reluctantly the surgeon acknowledged Aaron was in pain although he could not understand why.

As Aaron continued to cry, it was finally decided to remove the plaster which covered him from waist to toe. When the plaster was removed, Aaron gave an audible sigh of relief and we were soon to see 'why'. There was a cut on Aaron's ankle which was inflamed and festering – the result of his ankle being 'nicked' when the plaster had been put on. Even then, the surgeon would not acknowledge any responsibility – no doubt fearing recriminations.

Our concern was never to apportion blame – we all make mistakes – but on more than one occasion we saw how, because of the compensation culture, the medical authorities shied away from 'holding their hands up'.

The hip operation was not a success, and when told that his left hip was also dislocated, we had no desire to subject him to further surgery. We were guided by our own doctor who explained that, as Aaron would never be able to support his own weight, the operation was not really necessary. He also gave us some wise advice – telling us not to subject Aaron to surgery unless it was definitely necessary. "Consider Aaron," he said, "not just the part of the body which is affected. Consider the whole person. If the proposed treatment will not bring lasting benefit to Aaron, don't go through with it." Very wise advice which we never forgot.

This advice was to be confirmed when we had an appointment with Consultant Paediatric Neurologist Dr Lewis Rosenbloom at Alder Hey Hospital in Liverpool. Having made one or two helpful suggestions regarding Aaron's medical care, he concluded by making the following statement: "In situations such as Aaron's, healthcare is only a minor contributory to the welfare of the individual disabled person. Much more it is the quality of care that they receive, and in Aaron's case this is particularly important." We had always seen his care as a partnership between us and the medical profession but this reinforced our determination to always give Aaron the best care we possibly could.

In May 2007, Aaron was admitted to hospital with a chest infection and for the first time he was placed on an adult male ward. This was something we were never altogether comfortable with, as, to all intents and purposes, Aaron was a baby on an adult ward. It was especially difficult for Pat, because on the children's ward she had a bed but on the adult ward she had to be content with a chair. Hospital wards – even at night – are not the quietest of places and Pat did well to snatch two or three hours of sleep. But this in no way belittles the nursing care Aaron received, as this was always excellent.

Aaron was placed on a BIPAP (Bilevel Positive Airway Pressure) machine – a non-invasive form of therapy which delivers air pressure through a mask, making it easier for patients to breathe. This is because it supplies the blood with oxygen and allows carbon dioxide to leave the lungs. The critical time comes when a patient is brought off the BIPAP – is he able to breathe unaided? Aaron was breathing nicely – even smiling – when on the BIPAP, but when brought off the machine he continued to struggle.

This meant there was the alarming possibility that Aaron would never be able to breathe unaided and then his future would be determined by the courts. This was something we desperately hoped would not happen – a court deciding whether Aaron was to live or die. The Italian consultant could not have been more compassionate and was in tears as he explained the situation to us. He assured us that he would give Aaron all the time necessary, to see whether he could breathe without assistance.

They were anxious days, but one Saturday afternoon I was having a break at a football match when I got a phone call from Joanna – the mask had been taken off and Aaron had been breathing unaided for an hour. This was the beginning of his recovery, and our hearts were full of thankfulness to the Lord.

There were to be other admissions to hospital, each accompanied by anxious days, and this was especially true in May 2011. Aaron's prognosis was very uncertain and having spent a sleepless night, Pat had been grateful for the professionalism and comfort of an Indian nurse.

As the nurse went off duty, Pat asked her, "Are you going home to bed?"

"No," she replied, "I am going to church."

"Which church?"

"Parr Street Evangelical Church in Kendal."

Pat was amazed, as that was the church where we were members. Rupel had only just come to the church and, due to my preaching engagements, we had not met before. We have met many times since, both in church and on hospital wards.

Again, Aaron made a good recovery and his timing was perfect. Pat had been invited to a Royal Garden Party at Buckingham Palace and I was to accompany her, but with Aaron being so ill we had resigned ourselves to not going. The Garden Party was on the Tuesday, but over the weekend Aaron made such good progress that we were told he could be discharged on the Monday.

Weeks before, Aaron had been booked into Martin House Children's Hospice, as we had arranged to spend a night or two in London. As it happened, we arrived at the hospice Monday afternoon and got the train to London on the Tuesday morning. We had an amazing afternoon at the Palace, stayed overnight in London and caught the train back to Leeds on the Wednesday morning. A memorable time. And all the more enjoyable as a week beforehand it did not seem possible that we would be able to attend.

There was to be another dramatic visit to hospital. In January 2012, I pushed Aaron in his wheelchair to the local garage in order to buy a newspaper. On the way back, the front wheels of his chair got lodged in a pothole; the wheelchair toppled over, and even though Aaron was strapped in, his face hit the ground and the wound began to bleed. I picked Aaron up, left his chair in the road and rushed back to our home.

Pat opened the door and was just as shocked by my appearance as she was by Aaron's. She cleaned Aaron's wound and then made me a cup of sweet tea. We contacted a retired paramedic across the road and, even though Aaron was smiling, he recommended that we would have him checked out at Westmorland General Hospital in Kendal. This we did, and though Aaron had a black eye, he suffered no ill effects. His father's shattered nerves took rather longer to recover!

CHAPTER FIVE

Manchester Hospitals

For the first eleven years of his life, Aaron was fed by mouth, even though this was often a laborious process. Normally, when we swallow food and drink, it moves down through the oesophagus into the stomach, but this is not the case if a child has gastro-oesophageal reflux. Food and drink moves down the oesophagus but instead of it all passing into the stomach, a mixture of food, drink and acid travels back up the oesophagus. This causes not only irritation to the lining of the oesophagus but when children breathe, some of the mixture gets into the windpipe (aspiration). It can also cause irritation of the lungs and chest infections.

At a relatively early age, it soon became obvious that Aaron had gastro-oesophageal reflux. This is not an uncommon condition but with Aaron it was greatly exacerbated by the twisted shape of his body. He was often distressed whilst feeding and increasingly was being admitted to hospital with chest infections and the possibility of pneumonia. As previously stated, we had no desire to subject Aaron to unnecessary surgery but an operation to address this condition became essential.

The operation is known as a fundoplication, where the sphincter is strengthened so that the stomach is less likely to allow food and drink to travel back up the oesophagus. This operation was strongly recommended by the nursing staff at Bleasedale House, by our own GP and by all the specialists we saw at different hospitals in Manchester.

Aaron was booked in for surgery in January 1999, but an outbreak of meningitis caused the operation to be cancelled and it was eventually rescheduled for February. This was to be at the Pendlebury Children's Hospital – an austere structure, based around buildings dating from the

Victorian era. The hospital, founded in 1829, was the first in the UK to treat only children. It was eventually replaced by the Royal Manchester Children's Hospital which opened in 2009 at a cost of £500 million.

The operation was on a Tuesday and it was an emotional moment as Pat and I escorted Aaron to the doors of the theatre. As is frequently the case, Aaron was longer in theatre than we expected and anxiety levels began to rise. But then, much to our relief, he was brought on to the High Dependency Unit. He had survived the operation, but then we were told the disappointing news: the operation had not been a complete success. Due to his body shape, the surgeon had managed a half but not a full fundoplication and this meant Aaron would still be at risk of aspirating food into his lungs. Thankfully, Aaron recovered well and was home just a week after having been admitted.

During the operation, Aaron had a gastrostomy tube inserted into his stomach so that, if the need arose, he could be fed by tube. Our hope had been that he would be able to be fed both by tube and by mouth but sadly this was not to be. From now on, Aaron would be 'nil by mouth'. To many people, this would have come as a blow but, as far as we could ascertain, it made no discernible difference to Aaron. Principally, food is fuel for the body but it is also something to be enjoyed, and Pat and I were sad that Aaron was now being denied this pleasure.

Aaron's profound scoliosis resulted in another visit to a Manchester hospital. Scoliosis reduces space for internal organs to develop and can cause breathing problems. Initially, the problem was addressed by Aaron being provided with a spinal corset. This was rather cumbersome and caused him to sweat in hot weather, but we persevered with it, hoping the corset would prevent his scoliosis from getting worse.

The ultimate treatment for scoliosis is spinal surgery, where the spine is straightened by using metal rods, attached with screws, hooks and wires. With this in mind, an appointment was made to see Consultant Spinal Surgeon Dr Brad Williamson in Manchester. He was a lovely man with whom we immediately felt at ease and we had a lengthy conversation regarding Aaron. He felt that Aaron was too frail to withstand major surgery and had a personal reason for saying so. The only child he had ever 'lost' was a child with complex needs similar to Aaron's. This had obviously impacted upon the surgeon and we very much appreciated his candour and advice.

Mr Williamson did not feel that Aaron's spinal corset was having any beneficial effect; with or without it, his scoliosis would not worsen. Pat and I were relieved to hear this, as we felt there were times when the corset made Aaron feel uncomfortable. Once out of the corset, his wheelchair had to be altered to reflect his new 'shape'.

CHAPTER SIX

Mother but also Nurse

From the day Aaron came to us, Pat was his mother, but perhaps what she had not appreciated was that she would also become his nurse, and over the years I came to admire the medical knowledge that Pat acquired. The following medications were amongst the many that Pat had to administer to Aaron: Gaviscon, Lansoprazole, Cisapride, Beclomethasone, Salmeterol, Salbutamol, Loratadine, Epilim, Clonazepam, Baclofen. To me, I confess, just names; but to Pat, medications that were vital to Aaron's wellbeing.

After his gastrostomy, Aaron was fed by means of a pump and it was important that timing and volumes of the feed were adhered to. On one occasion, we had to bring Aaron home prematurely from a respite centre because he was suffering from sickness and diarrhoea. It transpired that Aaron had been overfed by a nurse who did not fully understand his feeding regime. The fact that Pat managed his pump feeds without mishap for over seventeen years is itself a testimony to her 'nursing' skills.

When Aaron was hospitalised, the nursing staff were always happy to leave his feeding and medication to Pat, indicating their confidence in her. This confidence was shared by our GPs who said that we knew Aaron far better than they did, and consequently were prepared to be guided by us when it came to things such as hospital admission.

I have a letter from Paul Gibson, Consultant Paediatrician at Royal Lancaster Infirmary, in which he states, "I am impressed with your increasing knowledge of health and lung function." Paul was an excellent paediatrician and we have nothing but praise for his commitment to Aaron and that of our GPs. In later years, we did sometimes contact the medical staff at Martin House, as they were the 'experts' in dealing with children like Aaron.

Due to our day-to-day contact with Aaron, we – and especially Pat – got to know his foibles and ways. Whenever he was agitated or uncomfortable, Aaron would hyperventilate, go rigid and his whole body would shake. The medics could never explain what was happening and understandably at times tended to overact. Twice when he was on respite, Aaron was admitted to hospital, and on another occasion, I was called to the hospital at three in the morning because Aaron was having an episode and all his monitor readings had gone haywire.

One March evening when Aaron was hospitalised, we were driving home to Ingleton in treacherous, icy conditions when we got an urgent phone call telling us there had been a rapid deterioration in his condition. We rushed back to the hospital to be met by apologetic staff – Aaron had settled down after another mysterious episode.

When this happened at home, Aaron would almost immediately return to normality if we raised his arm and put his cap over his eyes. Consequently, whenever we left him at Martin House, the hospital or with anyone else, these were almost always our parting words: "If he is being silly, raise his arm and put his cap over his eyes." We were never given a medical reason as to why 'arm' and 'cap' remedied the situation, but it worked and that was all that mattered.

Aaron's asthma and chest problems were always our greatest concern and Pat soon became proficient in the use of inhalers and nebulisers. I recall one Saturday being in Selkirk when Aaron was subject to an asthma attack. We rushed into a cafe and the owner kindly let us 'plug in' the nebuliser. In later years, we always travelled with portable oxygen tanks in Aaron's vehicle, but thankfully, we rarely had to use them.

Aaron was also doubly incontinent, and this caused nursing demands in other areas. Whenever we were out for the day, we took a change of clothing with us, as Pat was determined that Aaron should always be comfortable and at the same time presentable. Despite always having to lie on the same side, Aaron never had any bedsores – and again this was a tribute to Pat. Nurses would call once a month to check on him and many would commend Pat for her care.

We always considered mouth care to be an important aspect of Aaron's treatment. His mouth was permanently open and this caused its own problems. Initially, pink sponge mouth swabs were provided by the NHS but these were later outlawed on Health and Safety grounds. This meant we had to purchase the swabs privately and no health professional was allowed to use them. This very much became my department and I used them several times a day to clean round his mouth and tongue. In the night, we would sometimes use the swabs, slightly moistened, to freshen his mouth.

Three times a year, Aaron had a visit to the dentist in Settle and regular appointments with the chiropodist in Bentham. The dentist commented that Aaron was her best patient because, due to his disability, his mouth was always opened and, being 'nil by mouth', his teeth were exemplary.

However, Aaron's mouth being open was a potential hazard. One hot Saturday afternoon, I was enjoying a cricket match in Kendal when I noticed a wasp hovering at the entrance to his mouth. I managed to swat it away but shuddered at the thought of what might have happened.

Chiropody appointments were really only for senior citizens, but because Aaron had a life-limiting condition, he was accepted as a patient. These appointments were in addition to periodic outings to orthotists, occupational therapists, physiotherapists, dieticians and others. It was easier when Aaron was at Bleasedale House, as many of these appointments were co-ordinated by the nursing staff, and clinics were held on the school premises. This arrangement obviously ceased once Aaron had left school.

There were other non-medical needs that we had to attend to and these too could prove challenging. For example, cutting his hair was never an easy exercise. Aaron could not sit up, and positioning him so as not to hamper his breathing was always difficult. Over the years, he was placed on his side, seated on my knee, or positioned over a wedge in order to have his 'short back and sides'. Our daughter-in-law, Sarah, had been a Saturday girl hairdresser, and when she was with us she gave him a more professional cut than he ever received from his parents.

Once a month we had to order Aaron's 'food' and this was quite a logistical exercise, although it did become a little easier once the system was computerised. We were also responsible for ordering incontinence pads, as well as supervising repeat prescriptions. Every month, I returned from the chemists in Ingleton with a box of medications under my arm, and we were always grateful to the pharmacists for their advice and support.

Pat was never happier than when she was being mother to Aaron and so was distraught when, on one occasion, she had to abdicate this responsibility. I was visiting in Morecambe and even though Pat had not been feeling too well, she decided to come with me. I left Pat and Aaron in the Arndale Centre, arranging to meet them an hour later.

Shortly afterwards, Pat knew she was going to be sick, and rushing into Wetherspoons, she left Aaron in the doorway and dashed upstairs to the toilet. It soon became apparent she would not be able to leave the toilet in the immediate future and she knew that Aaron was unattended.

Pat tried my mobile but I was not answering and so she rang our daughter in Leeds, explaining her predicament and asking Joanna to telephone Wetherspoons in Morecambe. This she did and the staff assured Joanna they would deal with the situation. Moments later, there was a knock on the toilet door with a staff member enquiring after Pat's health and setting her mind at rest about Aaron.

Joanna eventually managed to make contact with me and I rushed to Wetherspoons, where Pat was still in the toilet but Aaron was 'propping up the bar'. It was a nasty bug, but eventually Pat emerged and we were able to travel home to Ingleton. We later wrote to Wetherspoons, thanking them for their care of both mother and child!

Andrew and Joanna became independent and 'flew the nest' but obviously Aaron never did. For almost twenty-nine years, Pat was his mother and nurse. People would sometimes comment, "It must be hard work," but neither Pat nor I ever saw it that way. We loved him, and so caring for his needs was just a part of our daily routine.

CHAPTER SEVEN

Social Workers

I have to be careful because my own daughter is a social worker, and I am certain that the number of social workers she met in her teenage years must have influenced her choice of career. In our experience, most social workers were dedicated, conscientious people, often trying to do an impossible and thankless task. With the breakdown of family life, it is social workers who so often are left to pick up the pieces.

My gripe was not with the staff but with the Social Services system and the 'politically correct / cover-my-back' policies under which the staff operate. A head of a Special School once unkindly commented, "If you haven't a problem, you don't need Social Services, and if you have, then they will make it ten times worse." Not, I am sure, a fair comment but one with which, at times, I was tempted to agree!

With Aaron being fostered for over sixteen years prior to adoption, it seemed there was a question that was never satisfactorily resolved: were we foster *carers* or foster *parents?* If a child only comes for a short stay, then the term 'foster carer' is perhaps appropriate, but surely this must change if a child is fostered long term or permanently.

There were occasions when we were gently reminded that we were Aaron's carers not his parents, but on other occasions Social Services were perfectly happy for us to assume parental duties. For example, when he had surgery in Manchester we signed the consent forms, but I am not certain we had the right to do so. However, no social worker would have wanted to travel from Lancaster to Manchester just to sign a consent form.

Due to the circumstances in which he was injured, Aaron was entitled to Criminal Injuries Compensation. This meant that he was awarded a sum of money which ensured that his housing and caring needs would always be met. In total, this took almost twelve years to materialise, and there was a continual march of medics, solicitors and even barristers through our house before Aaron eventually received his compensation. Social workers guided us through the process and, in general, they were very helpful. Or rather, they *were* helpful – until the money needed to be spent.

In winter, the cold wind off Ingleborough came right through our front door at 10 New Village and, to her credit, a social worker recommended that it would be beneficial to Aaron if a porch was fitted. A local builder assessed the work and gave me what I considered to be a reasonable quotation. I approached the Court of Protection, which was administering Aaron's compensation, and the Court agreed that the work could proceed. So far, so good, but then Social Services intervened and there was merit in what they were saying: if a front porch was a necessity, it was not right that Aaron should have to pay for it out of his own money; it should be financed by Social Services. Pat and I saw the logic of that and readily agreed, but the trouble was, Social Services never had sufficient money and so the proposed front porch could not go ahead. We were constantly assured that Aaron's care was paramount, but such an episode made us question whether this was always the case in practice.

In 1999, Joanna graduated from Bradford University and the graduation ceremony was on a Friday afternoon. Joanna was keen for Aaron to be at the ceremony, but this would have meant him coming out of school and us having to have special tickets. In the circumstances, we thought it best to just attend the ceremony ourselves and then to take Joanna out for a celebratory meal afterwards.

Several weeks prior to the date, I contacted Social Services, explained the situation and asked if they could provide two to three hours of after school care for Aaron. I heard nothing from them, but two weeks before the graduation, I was speaking with a friend who, besides being an ordained minister, was also the schools' doctor for North Yorkshire. As his home was in Silsden – on the route to Bradford – he told us to drop Aaron off and he and his wife, a qualified nursery nurse, would care for him.

Pat and I were grateful for this 'solution' to our problem and I notified our social worker. I did not get too positive a response but thought nothing about it until, shortly afterwards, she rang me back.

"I am sorry," she said, "but you cannot do it."

"Why not?" I asked.

"Because," she explained, "your friend has not been police-checked."

"Not been police-checked!" I spluttered. "He is the schools' doctor for North Yorkshire!"

"He has not been police-checked by *us*," she responded.

There were times when my sanctification was sorely tested and this was one of them! I proceeded to tell her that I was not happy with the decision and would be taking the matter further. The next morning, the social worker telephoned to say that on this one occasion, they were prepared to make an exception but it would be an isolated case.

I fully understand child protection issues and the safeguards Social Services must have in place, but surely common sense must come into the equation. It seemed that they were saying that Aaron must never be left with anyone who had not been police-checked by them. In practice, this was unworkable as, for example, there had been times when we had been on holiday with my brother and his wife, and Pat and I had gone out for a meal whilst they had looked after Aaron. They had not been police checked – were we doing wrong?

As parents with our own children, we had always made an assessment before they went for a short or a longer stay to someone's house and we wanted to be able to use the same criteria with Aaron. I suppose it came back to what I have already mentioned: officially we were his carers not his parents. After this, I never had quite the same confidence in Social Services and was tempted not to be as open with them in the future. After all, what they did not know about, they would not worry about.

I confess I have a lot of negativity when I think about Social Services, and when Aaron was adopted, it was a relief to have them 'off our back'. However, I repeat again, this is not to say there were not some outstanding social workers, and friendships made many years ago continue to this day.

CHAPTER EIGHT

Bleasedale House School

It had been a battle to get Aaron into Bleasedale House School but we never had any doubt that we had made the right choice. From the day he started, aged four, to the day he left, aged eighteen, the care, love and 'education' he received was first class.

Bleasedale House is an impressive building with a coach house and extensive gardens. It dates from 1860 and was a Red Cross Hospital and a Convalescent Home during the First World War. Lancashire County Council acquired the building in 1948 and now it is a day and residential school for children with PMLD.

There were four classes, one of which was a Further Education class for sixteen-to-eighteen-year-olds. As many of the children boarded at the school, there was also a residential curriculum with evening and weekend activities. Throughout his time at the school we were impressed by all of Aaron's teachers, and the regular day-to-day contact we had with them meant that though they were his teachers, they also became our friends.

In order to secure education funding, the school had to adhere to the National Curriculum and though, at first, it was strange to think of Aaron being taught mathematics, history, science etc., we came to see the value of it. It was a testimony to the skill and ingenuity of the staff that they could present different subjects in a relevant and meaningful way. The following are just some examples:

- *Science* – the understanding of forces by being pulled and pushed on a blanket.

- *Geography* – a visit to Brackenthwaite Farm where lambs were fed and horses stroked.
- *History* – the making of belts, shields and helmets used by the Vikings.
- *Design Technology* – the making of a Mother's Day card, using fabric paint on linen.
- *English* – by means of visual and tactile resources, adapting a scene from *Wind in the Willows*.
- *Maths* – using a range of equipment to play a variety of games with numbers.
- *Art* – experimenting with a variety of tools such as garlic presses, graters, lollipop sticks and pastry pickers.
- *R.E.* – participating in a sensory production of the Creation.

These are examples of how, in imaginative ways, the school followed the National Curriculum.

If there was a slight downside, it was this: because a child was doing the National Curriculum and receiving written reports as to their progress, some parents were perhaps tempted to assume that their child was more academically able than they were. We were never under any such illusion but were always profoundly grateful for the 'education' that Aaron was receiving.

However, Bleasedale House was far more than just an 'educational' establishment, because his medical and physical needs were also catered for. Aaron had access to various therapists and every week he used the hydrotherapy pool.

Birthdays were always celebrated at Bleasedale House and Aaron's eighteenth birthday was a special occasion. A party was organised with balloons, streamers and music, and I even took to the floor for a 'wheelchair disco'! It was a memorable evening – principally because it was Aaron's birthday but also because Andrew came down from the North-East with Sarah, confirming, as we had suspected, that they were more than just good friends!

The school may only have had twenty to twenty-five pupils but it employed well over a hundred staff. These included teachers, special support assistants, midday welfare assistants, residential social workers, nurses, therapists, care assistants, school secretaries, cooks, laundry workers and site supervisors. The significance of the numbers came home to me when, as a member of the governing body, I had responsibility for staff appointments.

Monday was my 'day off' from the church, but many Mondays were spent over at Bleasedale House conducting staff interviews. This was tiring and increasingly frustrating work. I enjoyed meeting the candidates but I found the interview rules very restrictive. No personal questions could be asked, no 'gut' feeling' taken into account; candidates had to be scored solely on the answers they gave to questions.

On one occasion, we interviewed an able young teacher but we had prior knowledge that due to her husband's work, she would only be in the area for one year. We could not ask her any 'personal' questions and consequently she was appointed because she was the outstanding candidate. The inevitable happened, and twelve months later we were going through the whole procedure again!

Each day, Aaron had an eighteen-mile, forty-minute journey from Ingleton to Silverdale. Lancashire County Council provided a driver and an escort – some of whom became personal friends. It had been suggested that Aaron could be a residential pupil, staying at the school from Monday to Friday. This was never something that Pat and I particularly wanted, as we were always happy to have Aaron at home with us. However, when he reached sixteen, we agreed that Aaron could stay on Thursday nights at the school. There were two reasons for this. There were times when, towards the end of the week, Aaron did seem tired and we felt it would be less taxing if he did board one night a week. We also knew that residential pupils had evening activities and as Aaron got older, we wished him to extend his 'social life'. This worked well for Aaron and for us, as it meant that Pat and I could, if we wanted, arrange something for a Thursday evening. For example, one December evening we were able to go with my brother and his wife to a Classic FM Carol Concert at Liverpool Cathedral.

There were occasions when, sadly, a pupil died and I was asked to officiate at the funeral. These were emotionally draining services but I trust that I was able to be of some help and comfort. It is my conviction that babies and all who do not have the mental capacity to understand the Gospel are covered by the blood of Christ. And for this reason, I was able to hold out the Gospel hope to grieving parents and relatives.

On a more joyful note, for a number of years I led the annual Christmas Carol Service held at the Gaskell Hall in Silverdale. We were joined by the Lancaster Salvation Army Band or the Lancaster and District Choral Society. One year, in such exalted company, Pat and I had the temerity to sing 'Starry Night' – a song which reached no. 34 in the hit charts of 1964, sung by The Joystrings. There was no danger of this 'cover version' having similar success!

CHAPTER NINE

Home/School Book

aron was not able to communicate but it was important that we and the school be kept informed of health issues, medical appointments, educational issues, school issues etc. This was resolved by a 'home/school book' in which we and the school gave a daily update regarding Aaron. Later it was titled 'My Diary' and we wrote in the first person. I tried to keep it informative and sometimes light-hearted, which I know was appreciated by the staff. A few extracts give a flavour of what we were saying:

Home/School Book

Monday. *Aaron has had a good half-term break. Last week, on successive days, he was in Lincoln, Sheffield, Derby and Manchester. He has probably come back to school for a rest – don't let him!*

John

Aaron has had a wonderful day. We have had a 'National Poetry Day' based on the theme 'journeys'. He's been on a jittery journey, a space journey, a magical journey and a train journey – all set to poetry. He's had a wonderful time and added on to Derby, Manchester, Lincoln and Sheffield, he's a well-seasoned traveller.

Marilyn

Friday. *Aaron dozed for a few minutes whilst having his bath, but then he did not get to sleep until 2am. Very strange behaviour. He did not seem in any way uncomfortable – just* not tired. It may catch up with him today. We hope he is alright.

John

Aaron has had a good day – surprisingly he has not nodded off. We have had lots of visitors today. Just up Aaron's street – ear wigging on others' conversations. Have a good weekend.

Marilyn

Wednesday. Aaron was agitated all evening and did not settle until after 11pm, when Pat gave him a paracetamol – difficult to know whether he was in pain or just tired. Hope he is alright on his trip to Preston today.

John

Aaron had a wonderful trip to Preston. Debenhams were superb with us. They cordoned off a section of the restaurant and arranged for Father Christmas to come. Aaron loved him, especially when he did a little dance and made his bells ring. Aaron got some good bargains for our tombola from a shop in the Fishergate Centre. A good day for us all.

Marilyn

<u>My Diary</u>

Monday. On Saturday I was guest at a wedding when Dad married a young woman. I don't mean that it was bigamy – Dad just conducted the service. I had an official photograph taken with the bride. Lovely, elegant, radiant – the bride didn't look too bad either.

Aaron

Wednesday. This morning I helped to cook lunch for everyone. I peeled the spuds and minced up the meat. After dinner, I went to the pool for a relaxing swim.

School

Monday. On Saturday I went to a football match in Liverpool. Dad said we were still in England but I'm not sure – they spoke a very funny language. On Sunday at church we *had a missionary from Peru. We all had lunch together and then he showed us slides of Peru. He also mentioned Chile, so I suggested turning up the heat.*

Aaron

Friday. *This morning I finished decorating my African plate. We then got wrapped up in our hats and scarves and went to look round the church. It was very nice with the sun shining through the stained-glass windows and the organ playing. In the afternoon, I did aerobics.*

School

Monday. *On Saturday morning, baby Joseph came to see me and we both fell asleep in front of the TV. Dad said we were like a couple of old men in a nursing home. The cheek of it. Dad is always dozing off in his chair and I tell him never to sit down when he visits the Nursing Home – he might end up being wheeled to the toilet!*

Aaron

Thursday. *This morning Green Watch Firemen came to school and brought their fire engine. I had a great time using the hose to water everywhere and tried the breathing apparatus. It was then time to go for a swim.*

School

Aaron was not able to return home from school and tell us what he had been doing, and he was not able to tell the school what we had been doing with him, but by means of the Home/School Book and My Diary, we were all kept informed.

CHAPTER TEN

Aaron Meets Royalty

S hortly after Aaron started at the school, I was appointed to be a Parent Governor. This was to be the beginning of almost ten years' service on the governing body – the last four as Chair of Governors. Much of the work I greatly enjoyed, but as more and more responsibilities were placed on governors, the role became ever more taxing and demanding. In 2000, I had to stand down as my health was starting to suffer.

However, in the summer of 1995, being a member of the governing body, I was told to keep Tuesday 26th September free. Initially, we were given no reason, but then we were told it was because there was the possibility of a royal visit. It was all 'hush hush' and no further details could be given.

Later, it was confirmed that the school was to have a visit from Her Royal Highness the Duchess of Gloucester, who was coming to open the Multi-Sensory Pool and the Sensory Room in the Residential Building. Aaron had been chosen – with Pat – to present a farewell gift to the Duchess as she left the school.

The Duchess was born in Denmark and married Prince Richard of Gloucester (cousin to the Queen) in 1972. Six weeks after their wedding, Prince Richard's elder brother, Prince William, was killed in a flying accident and Prince Richard unexpectedly became heir apparent to the dukedom. Upon the death of his father in 1974, the couple became the Duke and Duchess of Gloucester.

The Multi-Sensory Pool was one of the outstanding facilities at the school and provided a relaxing environment for pupils and outside user groups. The warm temperature – 36 degrees – encouraged muscles to relax and eased pain and discomfort in joints, making it easier to exercise. A sound system and lights added to the atmosphere and could be set up for livelier aerobic-type exercises. Such a facility was worthy of being opened by a royal visitor.

Several weeks were spent looking for an outfit suitable for Pat, and eventually we found one. Aaron, too, came under the sartorial scrutiny of his mother, and shirt, tie and trousers were purchased. However, having quite recently bought a new suit, I was quietly confident that Pat would not want any further expense. I could not have been more wrong! She assured me there was no way in which I was going to meet the Duchess without a new suit. I held out for as long as possible, but with family tensions rising, I succumbed on Monday 25th September. For some reason we were in Southport, and the deed was done.

In future years, this proved to be a good sermon illustration when preaching on 'The Man Without the Wedding Garment' in Matthew chapter 22. I could not appear in the presence of royalty just as I was – I needed a new suit. Similarly, we cannot appear before God 'just as we are' because "all our righteous acts are like filthy rags" (Isaiah 64:6). We each need that new suit which God Himself provides when we come to faith in His Son: "For he has clothed me with garments of salvation and arrayed me in a robe of his righteousness..." (Isaiah 61:10).

The great day came and we arrived at the school to be greeted by Special Branch Officers and sniffer dogs. The visit was being carried out with military precision and we were told when the royal car had left the motorway and how many minutes it would be before it reached Bleasedale House. Quite a crowd of onlookers had gathered at the entrance to the school but they got no more than a quick glance, as the car sped into the grounds and the gates were shut.

As Vice Chairman of the governing body, I was in the welcoming party and had the honour of being introduced to the Duchess. We had previously been instructed as to the required etiquette when meeting a royal visitor: greet with a small bow; shake hands only if the hand is extended; not to speak unless she spoke to you and then to address her as 'Ma'am' (the written notification helpfully clarified, "Ma'am as in Spam").

Shortly afterwards, all the local dignitaries were seated by the hydrotherapy pool, ready for the official opening, and I found myself sat next to Sir Mark Lennox-Boyd, MP for Morecambe and Lunesdale.

We chatted about the school and he was greatly impressed with the sounds and sights of the pool.

There was a forty-five-minute lunch break, for which a buffet had been provided by the school. This was a somewhat nervous gathering as we had been told that the Duchess might mingle amongst us. In the event, this did not happen as the Duchess and her lady-in-waiting retired to another room. It would have been nice to have had a conversation with her but I can understand her need for rest and refreshment during a busy day.

It was a beautiful autumn day and after lunch the Duchess was shown round the extensive gardens. The day passed all too quickly, and in no time at all Aaron was presenting the Duchess with a painting of the school. We were all most impressed by our royal visitor; her demeanour was such that everyone felt relaxed in her presence, and Pat found her genuine interest in the children heart-warming. It was a day when her attention was focused on the children and not on the local VIPs; a day which, sadly, Aaron would never remember but one that we would never forget.

CHAPTER ELEVEN

Aaron is Adopted

Initially Aaron came to us for one year, but the years passed by and he was permanently fostered. In reality, there is no such thing as 'permanent fostering' because at any time Social Services could have removed Aaron from us. For many years, we had felt that Aaron was part of our family, and knowing his birth mother wanted us to adopt him, we decided to make a formal application. By now Aaron was approaching sixteen and we knew that any application had to be made before he reached the age of eighteen.

We anticipated no problems but we had reckoned without the intransigence of Social Services. In fairness, almost all of the social workers we knew were supportive and encouraging, but on being shown a leaked document, there was one social worker who was opposing the adoption. This was a man who, for reasons unknown to us, had in the past proved aloof and difficult. His objection appeared to be that we were too old to adopt a multi-handicapped child. This was a feeble excuse, as we were only in our mid-fifties and it was surely to our advantage that we had sixteen years' experience of caring for Aaron.

Weeks went by with no definite yes or no from Social Services, and knowing how frail and vulnerable Aaron was, we were concerned that he might die without ever having been adopted. We shared this concern with our paediatrician and he wrote to Social Services, asking them to expedite the application. There was no meaningful response and we were left with no choice but to engage our own solicitor.

A solicitor was recommended and from our first appointment we knew that we had made the right choice. She had previous experience of Social Services and had crossed swords before with the very social worker who was proving obstreperous. She almost seemed to relish doing 'battles' with him again. Things now moved apace and on 2nd April 2004 we had to appear before Judge Mahon to hear his ruling.

Andrew and Joanna took the day off work and travelled over for the morning hearing. We were also thankful to have the support of a Christian friend, Brian Ventress. Brian was a police officer and elder of Grace Baptist Church in Lancaster, and was interested in Aaron because he had been on duty, sixteen years earlier, when Aaron's father had been brought into custody. Sadly, Brian died some four years later, at the early age of fifty-eight.

We were nervous as the Judge appeared, but within minutes the waiting was over. "You have cared for Aaron for the last sixteen years," he said. "Continue to do what you have been doing." What a relief – and how thankful we were to the Lord as friends, our solicitor and social workers embraced us and celebrated with us.

In 2016, I was reading the obituary of Judge Mahon and I saw the goodness of the Lord in that he was the judge we had appeared before. It said this: "He was a great judge because he listened, because he was compassionate, because he cared for his fellow human being and because he believed not only in justice but in doing right." In the providence of God, there was no more appropriate judge we could have come before.

Bleasedale House shared our joy and had soon arranged an adoption party. This was a most happy occasion, with plenty of balloons and music. The music was provided by Pete Moser and his one-man band. In 1988, Pete became the fastest one-man band in the world, running 100 metres in 19.75 seconds, playing 139 instruments, wearing five colours and playing four recognisable tunes. He did not attempt a world record at the adoption party but kept the adults and children fully entertained.

We were often asked whether *we* had chosen the name Aaron, as it was not a common name in the 1980s. Aaron had, in fact, been named by his mother and we were intrigued to know why she had hit upon this Old Testament name. We were somewhat dumbfounded to be told that she had been given a book of baby names and Aaron was the first name in the book! He was originally Aaron Linton but we decided to change Linton and, at my mother's suggestion, he became Luke.

Can an adoptive child ever mean as much to you as your own natural children? If that question had been put to me thirty years ago, I might have been undecided. Put that question to me today and my answer is unequivocal: the love we had for Aaron when he was alive and the pain we have felt since he died – there is the proof that in every sense *Aaron was our son.*

Adopting Aaron brought home to me, as never before, the wonder of being the adopted child of Almighty God. On 2nd April 2004, Aaron took our name, our address; he became our child and – for what it was worth – the inheritor of all that we possessed. In June 1969, through faith in Jesus Christ, I became the adopted son of God – and that is even more amazing. By nature, we are the children of the devil but, through grace, God has adopted us into His family. We all needed a Father, but God did not need any more sons because He already had a Son who was perfect and the apple of His eye. How amazing that He should adopt us and grant us a change of name, a change of address, a change of status. We are now called Christians; heaven is our home, and as the children of God, we are joint heirs with Jesus and the possessors of innumerable riches. Believers are adopted – not fostered – into the family of God. It is not a temporary but a permanent arrangement.

Once Aaron was adopted, we could now turn our attention to another pressing issue. Since moving to Ingleton in 1979, we had been happily settled in a three-bedroom terraced house, and with Andrew and Joanna having 'flown the nest' it was more than adequate for our needs. However, there was a problem. Aaron's breathing was so much easier when he was laid on his side rather than when he was sat up in his chair. Consequently, it was decided that he should have a wheelchair in which he could lie down. This was of great benefit to him, but the downside was that the wheelchair was so big that it was almost impossible to move him from room to room.

An extension had been built on at the back of the house and the en suite bedroom had proved to be of great assistance. It did not, however, deal with the 'wheelchair' problem. Another disadvantage was that Aaron's bedroom was downstairs and ours was upstairs. One night – half asleep – I came down to attend to him and ended up at the bottom of the stairs. I had knocked myself out and when I came round, I was looking into the face of a paramedic. Decision taken – we needed a more suitable house.

As pastor of the Evangelical Church, it was important that we stayed in the village. But weeks and months went by with nothing coming on the market. However, one morning I was out walking – having my 'quiet time' – when I saw a house which had just gone up for sale. Immediately, I had the feeling, *this is the house for Aaron.*

"I've found a house for us," I said to Pat.

"You are joking..." was her far-from-positive response.

"No," I said, "it is called Westgate and is on Croft Road."

Now there was no holding Pat back, and within the hour she had made an appointment with the estate agent. The irony was that Aaron had just started with a chest infection and so Pat and I had to view the house independently. From first seeing it, we fell in love with Westgate, and though it needed alterations, we could see it was the ideal house for Aaron. We explained to the estate agent that as far as we were concerned, we wanted the house, but the final decision would rest with the Court of Protection. On making contact with the vendors, they were keen that, if at all possible, we should purchase the property.

Two days after viewing the house, Aaron was admitted to hospital and for several days his condition was a cause for concern. Though anxious about him, Pat and I had a 'peace' – for surely, having waited so long for a suitable house, the Lord would not now take Aaron from us. Happily, he made a slow but good recovery.

My experiences with the Court of Protection had not always been happy ones, but again we were about to witness the providential goodness of the Lord. In the past, I had never been able to deal with a 'named person' as the staff changed with rapid regularity. This was my concern as I contacted them about the house purchase. Amazingly, the man allocated to us not only could not have been more supportive, but also stayed on the case right until the house was fully purchased.

Considerable work had to be done on the house, and this included the widening of doorways, the installing of overhead tracking, providing a porch and making a ramp for the back door, as well as creating a sensory garden. It was to be a year before the work was completed, but on 29th April 2005 we moved into Westgate.

This was the Lord's provision and made caring for Aaron much more manageable. With the hoists and overhead tracking, Pat could now bathe and dress him, even if I was not available. Our bedroom was just across from Aaron's and this made night times so much easier.

In 2015 we had a conservatory added, and in his last winter Aaron enjoyed being in there when the weather outside was unsuitable.

Westgate was a godsend and was to be his home for eleven years, until he went to a far better home in heaven.

CHAPTER TWELVE

Family and Friends

Throughout his life, Aaron had both his birth family and his adoptive family. For obvious reasons, we never met his natural father but we learned that having served his prison sentence, a year or two later he was found dead from a drug overdose. Relatives hope that prisoners will be drug-free when their loved ones are discharged, but this is seldom the case as drugs are often readily available in prison.

We had regular contact with Aaron's mother right until the time when he was adopted. She encouraged us to adopt him but perhaps felt she ought to 'stand back' once Aaron was officially ours. Having come off drugs, she married a supportive young man and Joanna was her bridesmaid. Pat and I, together with Aaron, were guests at the wedding. Aaron received cards on his birthday and at Christmas from an uncle and aunty – the uncle worked at the hospital where Aaron was treated and always showed an interest in him.

We only met Aaron's paternal grandmother on one occasion, but she often telephoned to enquire after him. She used to ring when about to visit her son in prison and we greatly respected the reason why she did. "When your boy is in prison," she said, "it is easy to feel sorry for him, so I need to be reminded of what he has done in order to keep things in perspective." A wise and mature approach.

We notified Aaron's birth family when he died and encouraged them to come to the funeral service. They were not able to attend because of age and sickness, but they sent a donation in his memory. We are thankful for the good relationships we had with Aaron's birth family and we felt for them in the very real pain experienced.

Andrew and Joanna accepted Aaron from the start and he was a well-loved uncle to all their children. Saul and Elodie – Joanna's children – had grown up with him and it was natural for them to moisten his mouth or even to empty his bottle. They knew that Uncle Aaron was different but they were never fazed by his disabilities – proof that children are very accepting if allowed to mix freely with the handicapped. From a very early age – whether tired or not – Saul and Elodie would 'hitch' a lift on his wheelchair.

As Aaron continued to defy the medics, there were family discussions as to what would happen if he outlived his parents, or if we got to an age when we were not able to care for him. Joanna was adamant that she would always care for Aaron and would never let him be institutionalised. Pat and I very much admired Joanna for her commitment to Aaron, as we knew that if the situation had ever arisen, she would have been as good as her word.

Aaron was loved by his families but also by a multitude of friends. When he died, we received almost four hundred cards – an indication of the impact he had upon people. Everyone knew him in Ingleton and he was also known by many through his long association with Bleasedale House School. My seven years of itinerant preaching also meant he had won many hearts through a wide area of northern England.

Ever since he was a baby, Pat had taken Aaron with her to women's meetings and so there were ladies in places such as Kendal, Reeth and Inskip who had shared the journey with us. They had a genuine interest in him, and before she shared a word at these meetings, Pat was usually asked to give an update on Aaron. On his birthday, for several years, we had an 'open morning' at Westgate, when we were joined by church friends and also friends from the village.

As an itinerant preacher, more often than not I was taking both morning and evening services, and this meant we required hospitality for the day. Without exception, Aaron was always welcomed with 'open arms' as our hosts went out of their way to ensure his comfort. Some, no doubt, had no previous experience of dealing with a multi-handicapped child, but their love for him banished any concerns they might have had. We shall ever be grateful to the Lord for the many kindnesses that Pat and I received, as Christian hospitality was graciously offered to us.

It was only rarely that Aaron received what Pat and I considered to be an unfriendly or negative response. Parents were sometimes embarrassed when their young children would blurt out, "What's the matter with him?" or, "Why has he got his mouth open?" We were never offended by such questions, recognising that young children are not known for tact and sensitivity. Pat used to ask the children if they had ever had a toy which had got broken and now did not work properly. She then explained that Aaron was broken and that is why he was in a wheelchair and his mouth was open.

There was an occasion when we received an invite to a wedding but Aaron was not included. We were not sure whether this was an oversight or was intentional. Sadly, when we made enquiries, we were to discover Aaron had not been invited because some of the guests might have felt his presence off-putting. In the circumstances, Pat and I did not feel that we could attend the wedding.

Thankfully, this was an isolated incident and over the years, Aaron was a welcome guest at weddings, wedding anniversaries, birthday parties, dedications, etc. It did, however, perhaps give us an insight into what handicapped people regularly experienced in less enlightened times.

Chapter Thirteen

Hobbies and Holidays

Is it possible for a child such as Aaron to have hobbies and interests? In one sense, no, but in the sense that certain things gave him obvious pleasure, the answer must be yes. Aaron was always happy and relaxed whenever he was riding in his vehicle or being walked in his wheelchair. Scarcely a day passed by without Aaron being taken for a drive, and Pat and I became familiar with back roads that we never knew existed.

Remarkably, though Aaron was often tired and drowsy, he never once dozed off when in his van. One memorable night, returning from the Carey Family Conference in Shropshire, we took a wrong turn and it was after midnight when we got back to Ingleton. Aaron, however, was still awake and smiling.

On our journeys, Aaron was usually smiling but I cannot say that was always true of his parents. One Thursday afternoon in early December 2011, we met Joanna in Ilkley to hand over Saul and Elodie, who had been staying overnight. As we set back for Ingleton – around 5pm – there were one or two flakes of snow in the air but nothing to concern us, until we got to Gargrave. It was now snowing heavily and we were in a long queue of stationary traffic. Apparently, the snowfall had caught the council unprepared and the gritters had not got out in time. Consequently, a lorry had jackknifed and others were not able to climb the road out of Hellifield. Aaron was due his medication at 6pm but we had not brought it with us, not expecting any delays.

There was no official information – only word of mouth – but one 'Job's comforter' assured us that there was no way we would get through to Ingleton that night. By now, the option of turning round and going to Airedale Hospital was not open to us as the road was blocked going in both directions. From time to time we edged forward, but so treacherous were the conditions, I skidded and collided with a fence.

Eventually the traffic did start to move and we finally arrived home at 10pm – a fifty-minute journey having taken five hours. Thankfully, although not medicated, Aaron suffered no ill effects and he certainly enjoyed the journey more than we did. From then on whenever we were going out, Pat took his medication with us, and from that winter onwards she insisted that I had a spade and blankets in the boot.

When he was younger and his wheelchair more manageable, Aaron enjoyed train travel. Many happy hours were spent on the Settle-Carlisle railway and though he could not appreciate the spectacular scenery, he nevertheless enjoyed the motion of the train. Sadly, when he had to lie on his side and a larger wheelchair became necessary, rides on trains were no longer practical. However, in June 2013, we were able to take him on the Rowsley-Matlock steam railway, as his wheelchair could go in the guard's van.

Whether it was the warmth of the sun or the breeze upon his face, Aaron was never happier than when out in the open air in his wheelchair. Old railway tracks turned into cycle paths and footpaths were especially suitable, and in Derbyshire we walked part of the Monsal and Tissington Trails.

Nearer to home, we were often to be found on the old Morecambe to Wennington rail track. Parks and promenades were also ideal for walks and we clocked the miles up with frequent walks in Grange-over-Sands and Morecambe. I suspect that many wheelchairs are only used to transport their users from one room to another, but this was never the case with Aaron's wheelchair. His had a considerable 'mileage' on it and consequently needed regular servicing.

His love of the outdoors meant that, when the weather was favourable, Aaron often accompanied me to football and cricket matches. He could not see much or understand what was going on but his smile confirmed that it was an enjoyable experience for him. Some Saturdays, I would drop Pat off at a shopping centre, then Aaron and I would go to a sporting fixture.

There were times when I was thankful that Pat was not there to see our escapades or else Aaron might not have had future permission to go with his dad. Having left Pat in Ormskirk, Aaron and I went down the road to Burscough to watch Burscough Bridge v. Ashton Athletic, but forty minutes into the match there was a cloudburst. So torrential was the rain that the referee took the players off the field, but Aaron and I were stranded in the middle of an open field. I had an umbrella and though I was soaked to the skin, I did manage to protect Aaron from the worst of the elements. Thoughtfully, the referee came over to see if we were alright before restarting the game.

On another occasion, Pat was in Brighouse town centre and I had taken Aaron to a match on the outskirts of the town. Unfortunately, the field could only be accessed through a narrow stile. Five of the home side, when made aware of my predicament, hoisted Aaron and wheelchair over a five-foot wall. Pat was shocked when told about it – what a mercy she was not there to actually see it!

When Aaron was eleven, we went to watch Kirk Deighton Rangers v. Robin Hood Athletic – I recommend such fixtures, which I consider to be far preferable to watching often overpriced professional matches. Prior to the kick-off, the referee came straight over to Aaron and confided that he had a five-year-old multi-handicapped son. He welled up as he told me that it was a twenty-four-hour commitment and he and his wife had not had a night out together since the child was born. It has been said, "Remember to be kind, everyone you meet is fighting a hard battle." How true that it is, even of referees, who are often the target of abuse from players and spectators.

One morning, I took Aaron with me to watch Everton U18s and among the spectators was ex-Liverpool supersub David Fairclough. David kindly agreed to be photographed with Aaron and we still have that picture today. For non-football aficionados, David played 153 matches for Liverpool, 61 as a substitute, and he gained a reputation for making an immediate impact.

Saturday afternoons in summer were often spent on the boundary edge, as we spent an hour or two at a cricket match. In the early 2000s, Andrew was captain of Richmondshire Cricket Club and sometimes Aaron would go to watch his big brother. The cricket professional at that time was the Sri Lankan 'Shani' Dissanayake and Andrew shared a house with him. 'Shani' had a disabled brother and when Aaron died, we were moved when 'Shani' telephoned from Australia to offer his condolences. Aaron, like his dad, was a Lancastrian, but on one occasion he did play truant to see Yorkshire playing at Headingley!

If the weather was favourable, we often wheeled Aaron round his multi-sensory garden. The path was made of different materials and

Aaron enjoyed the vibrating of his wheelchair. In the summer months, Aaron was with me whenever I cut the grass – the noise of the mower causing him to smile. We had a gazebo which we erected in the garden and, sheltering from the sun, Aaron smiled or dozed as I read the newspaper.

Aaron obtained great pleasure from music and to see his smile was always heart-warming. In church his face lit up whenever we were singing and therefore it was appropriate to sing four rousing hymns at his funeral service. In summer we would from time to time take Aaron to brass band concerts – this was no hardship as I have always had a love of such music. Whether in Happy Mount Park in Morecambe or in the gardens of the Hark to the Bounty in Slaidburn, I was stirred by the music and I am sure Aaron was as well. There was always music in his bedroom, not Radio 1 or 2 but chiefly Classic FM, gospel music and brass bands.

In the mornings, we often placed Aaron in front of the television. It was not that he could understand the programmes but he did seem to gain enjoyment from the noise and changing pictures. This meant Pat and I could continue whatever we were doing, knowing that Aaron was occupied.

When Aaron was eight months old, he went into Alexander House for a week whilst we had a holiday in the Lake District. We enjoyed the break but greatly missed Aaron, and other than for three days in the Cotswolds and two forty-eight-hour dashes to Switzerland, we never holidayed again without him.

We chose our holiday accommodation with care as, in case of an emergency, we never wanted to be too far from the hospital in Lancaster. This did not restrict us too much as we rented cottages in South West Scotland, Northumberland, Yorkshire, Lincolnshire, Derbyshire, Staffordshire, Shropshire and North Wales. None of these cottages had disabled facilities but we improvised as best we could. That is not to say there were not unexpected hazards. We once rented a converted granary in Lincolnshire, which could only be accessed by means of twelve external steps. This put great stress on my back as I carried Aaron up and down the steps, but not as much stress as it placed on Pat, witnessing the procedure.

Our normal holiday routine was to leave a cottage at 10am, returning some five hours later, having had our main meal out. On the last three holidays we had with Aaron, we were accompanied by our daughter and her family. This made thing easier as there were additional pairs of hands to help with his transportation. Even then, things did not always go smoothly. Carrying Aaron upstairs in Northumberland, I stumbled and broke a spindle in the staircase. Fortunately, my son-in-law Al is very practical and after a visit to the local hardware shop, the staircase was returned to its former glory.

Whilst staying in Shropshire, we visited the Percy Thrower Garden Centre in Shrewsbury. I got Aaron out of his van but when I turned round... he was not there. His wheelchair had run down a slope and his 'great escape' had only been foiled by a hedge. We were somewhat shaken and yet at the same time thankful, as without the hedge the situation could have been much more serious.

Shrewsbury is a lovely town and yet, where Aaron is concerned, it does not hold the happiest of memories. A year or two earlier we had been on holiday with my brother and his wife and decided to have an afternoon trip on the River Severn. I had to hold Aaron in my arms and I can only think that I was holding him too tightly, as the colour began to drain from him and his breathing was affected. We were glad when the 'cruise' came to an end and again thankful that Aaron soon recovered.

Due to Aaron not being well, we had to cancel a cottage in Scotland, and the last time we went to Staffordshire we had to return home early. This made us decide that in the future we would only book a cottage if Jo and her family were able to come with us. In the event of Aaron not being well, they could still have the benefit of the holiday. For shorter breaks and when I was preaching at a distance from Ingleton, we used Premier Inns and found that their family rooms fully met our needs.

In the early 2000s, we went four times to the annual Carey Family Conference at Cloverley Hall in Shropshire. Aaron was a popular guest and participated each year at the Thursday night 'Entertainment Evening'. He was first on the 'bill' as Pat recited a poem which I had composed for him. Sadly, the disabled facilities were somewhat limited and this was the reason we had to stop going.

It was through a contact at the Carey Family Conference that we were asked to write a full-page article about Aaron for Grace Magazine. This we did and it was published in the August/September 2004 edition. Shortly afterwards, we were having a meal in Lancaster when a young woman approached us and asked, "Is this Aaron? I've just been reading about him in Grace Magazine." She was working in the city, and there in Sainsbury's restaurant – because of Aaron – we were able to have a profitable time of fellowship.

The longest distance we ever travelled with Aaron was in October 2013 and 2014 when I was speaker at the Christian Endeavour Autumn Break in Cardiff. We were nervous about taking him such a distance but we need not have been. On the way down, we broke the journey, but on the Friday, we journeyed straight back from Cardiff to Ingleton.

The first year when we got to our accommodation there was a notice in the foyer indicating which rooms had been allocated to us. Our room was no. 11 and against Aaron's name were written the words "no food / no bed". No food was applicable as Aaron was fed through a tube, but though he spent his days in a wheelchair, he did require a bed at night. We gently pointed this out to the Centre Manager and he immediately arranged for a bed to be provided. It was a reminder that no such arrangements were made for Jesus. He was hungry in the wilderness, hungry at Bethany and He, for whom there was no room in the inn, had no guarantee of a bed at night. It was a life of continual self-denying and suffering.

Aaron was a familiar face in a number of cafés, garden centres and supermarkets. After his death, it was not always easy to revisit some of these places as, invariably, staff asked after him and this could be quite upsetting. Nevertheless, it brought home to us just how much Aaron had been loved and we much appreciated the sympathy and love we received.

Some places we have not yet been back to, as their association with Aaron is still raw. Hellifield Railway Station was a particular favourite, and many a lunchtime was spent in the tea rooms. December 2015 was particularly memorable, when the station hosted a Christmas Music and Carol Evening with Settle Voices. Aaron's face was a picture and it is a memory of his last Christmas that we will always treasure.

CHAPTER FOURTEEN

Aaron Leaves School

In this life 'all good things come to an end' and in July 2006, after fourteen happy years – March 1992 to July 2006 – Aaron got to school-leaving age.

A signed book with contributions from all the staff was presented to him and it reveals something of the impact that Aaron had made upon them.

Here are some excerpts from the book:

"All the best. We will miss your lovely smile."

"Have a great adulthood. We will miss that great smile of yours."

"Wishing you all the very best for the future. I will definitely miss your great smile and giggle."

"To Mr Mollitt – junior. I am missing you already. Keep smiling."

"You have been a superstar through thick and thin. Your smiles and laughter will always be special. Take care. Keep your Mum and Dad in order (if you can)."

"To my very best swimmer. I will miss you loads."

"We go back a long way. It only seems like yesterday when you came into my class, starting school for the first time. You were a star then and you will remain one."

"Whenever I am feeling down, I see that big smile and you cheer me up. Who will do this in September? Will miss you."

"I have lots of memories of our Food Technology lessons in Class 2. Every week, without fail, you used to be covered with food or water. All you could do was laugh."

"Who would have thought you would have grown into such a mature young man? It has been a pleasure to work with you and you will be a greatly missed member of the class. September is going to be very dull without you and your weekend news."

"Have a happy future and keep smiling. Your smile brightens any room and melts many hearts. I'll miss you."

"Keep that beaming smile which entertains us all."

Well over fifty staff contributed to the book and almost all mentioned his infectious smile.

Once a pupil reaches the age of sixteen, Bleasedale House places great emphasis on preparing students for life after school. Links are formed with student transition workers and there is close liaison with appropriate post-school placements. We have nothing but praise for the efforts made by the school, but North Yorkshire Adult and Community Services left a lot to be desired. There was nothing in place when Aaron left school, and six months later, there was still nothing on the horizon.

A letter from NYCC dated 6th December 2006 gives a hint of what we were facing:

Dear Mr and Mrs Mollitt,

I would like to take this opportunity to update you with regards to the services that we are seeking to provide for Aaron.

With regard to Aaron attending day services at Duke Street, Settle. The manager _____ _____ has a copy of Aaron's health action plan which he will be looking at to ensure that the staff at Duke Street have the skills and training to care and support Aaron correctly and safely. There is a query around the possibility of staff having to undertake some care which would be classed as nursing intervention; this is in relation to the possibility of Aaron's colostomy tube coming out and having to be replaced. Nevertheless, we are working to resolve any issues.

I have applied for funding in order for Aaron to have one-to-one support to attend Duke Street if this is deemed necessary and to support him to access the community and possibly hydrotherapy, enabling Aaron to increase his social inter-action and provide you with some respite.

Unfortunately, I have only been working with the team on a temporary basis but a permanent Transitions Manager has now been appointed. I apologise that due to changes in staff we have been unable to provide continuity.

Yours sincerely,

This letter was only written because our daughter, Joanna, had expressed her concern that nothing had yet been provided for Aaron. It reveals what I so often saw to be the weakness of Social Services: lack of funding, lack of trained staff, constant changes of personnel.

Pat and I, together with Aaron, had visited Duke Street but it was not encouraging to find that there was no disabled access. We had to go round to the rear of the building and then, not without some difficulty, it was just about possible to access the property. This is not to criticise the staff or the good work done for many at Duke Street but it was a facility totally unsuitable for Aaron.

Two months later, I wrote to NYCC stating that after well over eighteen months of frustration and inactivity, we had decided not to continue with the Adult and Community Services and would make our own arrangements. In their defence, children such as Aaron had never been expected to reach school-leaving age and I suspect this is why it was difficult to make adequate provision for him.

This was not an easy decision but the next ten years were to prove that it was the right decision. It meant we had to make certain sacrifices but the gains far outweighed the losses. Up to October 2009, I was still the full-time pastor of Ingleton Evangelical Church and I had no intention of 'short changing' my congregation. Consequently, I would start work an hour or two earlier in the morning or work into the evening, so that I could devote time to Aaron during the day. There were, however, numerous occasions when, visiting hospitals or the homes of church members, Aaron came with me and I think there were times when patients and 'parishioners' were more pleased to see him than they were to see me!

On taking semi-retirement in 2009, I could be much more 'hands on', and bathing and dressing Aaron became part of my daily routine. Many afternoons were spent in cafés, garden centres, National Trust properties or, if the weather was favourable, taking Aaron for a walk. Pat and I are grateful to the Lord for the many precious memories we have of happy times spent with Aaron in his post-school years.

CHAPTER FIFTEEN

Martin House

Our GPs were always fully supportive, and as Aaron got older and approached school-leaving age, they were anxious that we should have access to respite facilities. Consequently, we were put in contact with Martin House Children's Hospice.

When Rev. Richard Seed moved from his parish in Oxford to Boston Spa in 1980, there was only one other established children's hospice in the world and that was Helen House in Oxford. Richard saw the need for a second such hospice in the north of the UK, and in 1982, he was approached by a number of Leeds-based paediatricians wanting him to be actively involved in providing a northern hospice for children.

Thus, the project began and four years later, in November 1986, HRH The Duchess of Kent laid the foundation stone, returning a year later as Patron to open the hospice. In the Mission Statement, Martin House states that its purpose is "to help children and young people with a life-limiting condition, along with their families, to live well and fully".

In 2005, we were visited by Mike Miller, the Consultant Paediatrician at the hospice, who assessed Aaron and confirmed that both he and we would benefit from the facilities they had to offer. We spent an afternoon at the hospice, were most impressed by what we saw and, thus, there began eleven years of happy stays for us at the hospice. This itself was highly unusual, as due to having a 'life-limiting condition', it was rare for a child still to be going to Martin House after eleven years.

We went regularly for four-or-five-night stays, four times a year, and it proved to be a godsend. We could have left Aaron but we always stayed with him, and during the day we would go off to Harrogate, York or Leeds. One of my regular treats was to have breakfast at The Tea Lounge in Tadcaster, where the fried egg in granary bread became my favourite.

The only time we did 'abandon' him was when Andrew and Sarah had twins in Switzerland and we went over for their first and second birthdays. We were only away for two nights and we knew that Aaron was having the best of care. Also, our daughter and family were just half an hour from the hospice and they came to see Aaron each day.

One of the memories we will always treasure is of returning from Switzerland to Martin House one Monday night, when Aaron was about to go to bed. I went up to him in his wheelchair, blew a raspberry and his face lit up with joy. Over the years, Aaron had given us many smiles but this was in a different category altogether, and in future visits the staff often commented on it.

Martin House does not just provide for the child and parents; the hospice 'ministers' to the wider family. Our grandchildren Saul and Elodie came to Martin House from being just a few days old and they revelled in this children's paradise. On occasions, Elodie came whilst Saul was at school, but it had to be a 'secret' visit or else Saul would not have wanted to go to school. With sandpits, bicycles, outdoor climbing frames and every imaginable toy, it is little wonder that the hospice is such a magnet for children.

In eleven years, the only drawback was the inevitability of putting on weight. The meals – produced by Robin the cook – were temptingly delicious, and with cakes and biscuits readily available, 'Slimming World' and 'Weight Watchers' were dirty words. Whenever wider family came to see Aaron, they were encouraged to stay to have meals and truly went away a 'wider' family!

Aaron's day began with a leisurely bath and then there were appropriate activities throughout the day: music sessions, the art room, walks in the grounds, TV programmes, videos, etc. A highlight was rabbits, guinea pigs, lambs or birds being brought into the hospice, which the children could hold and feed. Sometimes we would walk Aaron into Boston Spa and have a scone and a coffee.

I treated Martin House as an opportunity to 'recharge my batteries' and spent much time reading in our bedroom. Sometimes in the evening, I indulged in my hobby of watching non-league football and would travel to grounds I could not have reached from Ingleton. Pat 'circulated' amongst staff and parents and found it to be an evangelistic opportunity. There were parents whose children had just died or were dying and she was able to speak of the eternal life to be found in Jesus. Many Asian families use Martin House and in sensitive ways Pat was able to share the Gospel with those of other faiths. Pat was also sometimes a 'listening ear' amongst the staff, and again Gospel opportunities presented themselves.

In September 2014, Radio York broadcasted their live news programme from Martin House, and Pat and I agreed to be interviewed. We had no prior knowledge of what questions would be asked but the presenter put us at ease, and before we knew it we were 'on air'. As far as we could judge, the interview went well and, in what we trust was an appropriate way, we were able to share our faith. Afterwards, a member of staff told Pat he was pleased we had mentioned our faith and this was a further opportunity for Pat to 'gossip the Gospel'.

Some people have the mistaken impression that hospices must be sad and morbid places but this was never the case with Martin House. True, there were sad times, but my abiding memory will be of the joy and positivity which the staff unfailingly displayed. They created a family atmosphere, a sense of belonging, and this is something we shall always remember with gratitude.

We shall greatly miss our regular 'forays' to Boston Spa but we hope to maintain some form of contact. The hospice movement is very much dependent on voluntary donations, and Joanna and family, having done sponsored runs for Martin House in the past, intend to do more in the future.

CHAPTER SIXTEEN

Sermon Illustrator

I have always found illustrations to be a vital component of preaching. If concentration is proving difficult, then an apt illustration can quickly refocus a congregation on what is being said. I have always favoured personal anecdotes rather than illustrations taken from a book, and this is where Aaron was to prove most useful. We had many escapades and experiences with him, which I was able to use to illustrate biblical truths.

When Aaron came to us as a ten-week-old baby, we were told that he had been baptised with water from the River Jordan. I presume, because of his injuries, it had been an emergency baptism. Whatever our views on infant baptism, the vital thing is not water gathered from the Jordan but the blood shed on Calvary. As the popular worship song says, "What can wash away our sins? ... Nothing but the blood of Jesus."

One bitterly cold March day, I was hurrying to get Aaron into his specially adapted van when, in my haste, having secured his wheelchair, I carelessly locked the car keys in the vehicle. This was a potentially serious situation as Aaron was prone to fitting and must have regular medication. We thought of ringing the RAC or a local garage but it was a Saturday afternoon and time was of the essence. Eventually, I said to Pat, "Why not ring the Fire and Rescue?" And that is what we did.

Within minutes, we heard a siren and a fire engine was with us. Four men jumped out, and when they heard of our predicament they could not have been kinder. They went to the state-of-the-art fire engine and emerged with – wait for it – *a wire coat hanger.* For over half an hour they attempted to open the door, but vehicle manufacturers today are wise to potential car thieves and all their efforts came to nothing. Eventually, they broke a side window and when the door was opened, there was Aaron smiling and none the worse for the experience. He had been rescued from a potentially serious situation.

Aaron did not realise the danger he was in. Similarly, in their sin and rebellion against God, men and women do not realise the danger they are in. Aaron, because of his multiple disabilities, was unable to do anything about the situation, and men and women are quite incapable of saving themselves. For Aaron to be rescued it needed outside intervention, and that is true for sinful men and women. Jesus came from heaven to earth to do for us what we could never do for ourselves. He came to die upon a cross to rescue us from our sins. Praise God for outside intervention!

Visiting a shopping mall one afternoon, we decided to have a coffee at a restaurant on the first floor. As Aaron was with us, Pat had to use the lift. Unexpectedly, halfway up, the lift stopped and Pat and Aaron were suspended between the two floors; not a desirable situation in which to find oneself but eventually the fault was rectified and the first floor was reached.

When Jesus died upon the cross, He was suspended between earth and heaven and that was significant. Earth did not want Him because He was pure and righteous and in His Presence, men felt dirty and unclean. Earth did not want Him and heaven would not have Him because Jesus was bearing "our sins in his own body on the tree"[1]. Rejected by earth and by heaven – how great was His suffering!

We may not know, we cannot tell,
What pains He had to bear;
But we believe it was for us
He hung and suffered there.[2]

---

[1] 1 Peter 2:24 (KJV)
[2] Cecil Frances Alexander, 1818–1895; *There Is a Green Hill Far Away,* verse 2.

When Aaron was in Manchester Children's Hospital for major surgery, Pat and I were understandably anxious as we accompanied him to the doors of the operating theatre. Why, as loving parents, were we subjecting our son to the pain of the surgeon's knife? There was only one explanation: it was necessary.

Why did God subject His Son, the apple of His eye, to the pain and humiliation of the cross? There is only one explanation: it was necessary.

There was no other good enough
To pay the price of sin;
He only could unlock the gate
Of heaven and let us in. [3]

Aaron was a help to me in my ministry in many ways, not least in providing me with a number of homely sermon illustrations.

---

[3] Cecil Frances Alexander, 1818–1895; *There Is a Green Hill Far Away,* verse 3.

CHAPTER SEVENTEEN

Final Days

Throughout his twenty-eight-plus years with us, Aaron had numerous chest infections and admissions to hospital were necessary. Several times he was dangerously ill, but on each occasion, he bounced back and showed no ill effects. Though we had been told it was probable that Aaron would not reach the age of ten, and then later, twenty, nevertheless the years passed by and his health and especially his breathing, rather than deteriorating, if anything, improved.

Consequently, when one Friday Aaron started with a chest infection, we were not too alarmed. Pat began treating him with steroids and antibiotics, and over the weekend we felt he was getting over the infection. A doctor who called on the Monday was satisfied that Aaron was responding and said that she would give us a ring on Wednesday.

However, during Monday night there was a noticeable change in his condition, and by 7am we had telephoned for the ambulance. I carried Aaron out, never thinking for one moment that he would not return. Pat travelled with him and later I went down to the A & E at Royal Lancaster Infirmary.

Initially, they were concerned about his condition, but the treatment began to have an effect and by early evening he had been allocated to a ward. Aaron always got a warm reception from the staff, many of whom had nursed him over many years. His bed was near to the nursing desk and though Pat wanted to stay the night, we were encouraged to go home and get some sleep. The hospital promised to contact us if there was any change in his condition during the night.

We were back down at the hospital before 8am but were rather disturbed when we saw Aaron. Despite being on the ventilator, he was still struggling to breathe and the demeanour of the staff indicated that they were concerned. This was expressed to us by a doctor later that morning, who assured us that everything possible was being done for Aaron. We did not move from his bed, hoping and praying that we would see some improvement. This did not happen, and though doctors and nurses were constantly at his bedside, it became apparent that they were running out of options.

During the morning, a friend had rung Pat, but she had not been able to answer as we were speaking with the doctor. Around 1pm, Pat intended to return the call but inadvertently telephoned another number and found herself speaking to the wife of Dr Kai. For a number of years, Kai was a member of our church in Ingleton, and I had the joy of baptising him. In the providence of God, Kai had Wednesdays off from his GP practice in Settle and when he heard about Aaron, he said he was coming to the hospital. It is a journey of well over an hour but he was on the ward by 3pm.

Kai was with us when the doctor indicated that there was nothing more they could do for Aaron and he would have to come off the ventilator. However, she wanted us to speak with Aaron's consultant before any action was taken. This was another example of providence, as his consultant just 'happened' to be on the ward.

Kai was again present as it was explained to us that Aaron *would* have to come off the ventilator but it was our decision as to when this happened. The consultant helpfully explained that the decision to remove the ventilator was not our decision but his clinical decision.

We telephoned Joanna, who at first indicated she wanted to come to the hospital. However, she was so distraught that we did not think it wise for her to make a two-hour journey. She had seen Aaron just six days before, when he had been all smiles, and we agreed it was better for her to have that memory of him. We then had to decide whether to take Aaron off the ventilator that evening or wait until the morning. It was here that we saw the goodness and the mercy of the Lord. At such times it is not always easy to absorb all that a consultant is saying, but it was wonderful to be able to talk it over with Kai – a doctor, a Christian and a friend.

Kai confirmed that Aaron's body was shutting down and there was nothing to be gained by keeping him on the ventilator. We conveyed our decision to the consultant and within minutes the ventilator was removed from his face. Pat and I hugged Aaron and I was given the strength to quote passages from Psalm 23, John 14 and Revelation 21. I committed Aaron to the Lord, and within twenty minutes of coming off the ventilator, his sufferings were over and Aaron was in the presence of the Lord.

The two nurses and young doctor who witnessed his passing were distraught, and in her grief Pat had to comfort them. It was 7pm and Kai, having given thanks for Aaron, committed us into the Lord's care and keeping. It was hard returning home that night and being faced with Aaron's empty wheelchair and bed. Our bedroom was across from his but that night I had to sleep in a bed upstairs.

It is amazing how quickly news travels; by the next morning – Thursday – we were already receiving cards, emails, phone calls and flowers. Andrew teaches in Singapore, but within hours of hearing that Aaron had died, he was on a plane and he was in our home by 10.30am on the Friday morning. We very much appreciated his coming and he was to be a real help and comfort during the eight days he was able to be with us. We wanted the funeral to take place reasonably quickly, as we knew that Andrew had to return to Singapore. Consequently, Aaron died on 18th May and the funeral was scheduled for 26th May at Bethel Chapel, Clapham.

We had a private interment at Ingleton Cemetery before the service at Clapham. The church was full, with many standing, and it was estimated that the congregation was somewhere in the region of three hundred. My brother Jim took the service, with Andrew reading the lessons and our grandson Saul reading a poem which he had written. Saul, who was seven, and his sister Elodie, aged six, were heartbroken as they had never known Nana and Granddad without Aaron.

Saul bravely read his poem: "Uncle Aaron loves his van. Nana and Granddad push him around. Climbing all over him. Loves to listen to music. Enjoys a jacuzzi bath. Always laughing. Always loves Martin House. Riding on his wheelchair. Our uncle Aaron is the best. Nieces and nephews love him." There was scarcely a dry eye in the church and Saul richly deserved the applause he received, as he read the poem on behalf of his sister and his three cousins, who were in Singapore.

I had written a tribute to Aaron and though I would have loved to have given it personally, I was too emotional to do so. Jim read it for me and we will always be grateful to him for taking the service as, at the time, he had his own health problems.

As I have said previously, Aaron always enjoyed singing and music, and this was reflected in the hymns that we chose. We began with 'How Great Thou Art' and ended with 'To God Be the Glory'. The singing was a 'foretaste' of heaven, with one unconverted man saying, "I didn't know people still sang in churches today. I have never ever heard singing like that." Jim gave an appropriate Gospel message and many were later to comment on what a 'wonderful' service it had been.

Pat and I were moved to know that a boy who never spoke had made such an impact on so many people. Settle Playbarn and Ingleton Playgroup closed as a mark of respect, and there were Christian friends from different churches in Cumbria, Lancashire and Yorkshire present at the service. Andrew had produced a book and slides on the life of Aaron and these were available as people partook of refreshments at Ingleborough Community Centre.

Donations in his memory came to £1,700 and these were equally divided between Martin House and Barnabas Fund. Barnabas Fund is a Christian organisation which does outstanding work in supporting persecuted believers throughout the world. In their acknowledgement, Martin House wrote thanking us for the donation "in memory of your incredible son. Everyone at Martin House feels privileged to have been involved in his care and we shall miss your family visits."

Chapter Eighteen

Lesson Learned

Over the twenty-eight years we were privileged to have Aaron, we were taught many things that, perhaps, we could not have been taught in any other way – things about ourselves, about a fallen world, but most of all, wonderful things about the goodness and mercy of our God.

Twelve months after Aaron came to us, we had a visit from his paternal grandparents and we were faced with a devastated, broken couple. They could not come to terms with the injuries that their son had inflicted on a baby boy and even though we tried to be as reassuring as we could, they could not disguise their pain and distress. John Donne said, "No man is an island," and how true that is. What we do does have a profound effect upon other people.

We can read about child abuse cases and yet never appreciate the impact it has upon the wider family. This is something we soon learned as we had contact with several members of Aaron's birth family. What we do – be it good or bad – does affect other people.

This is a hard world but it would be even harder if everyone was strong in body and sound in mind. This was brought home to us again and again in kindnesses shown to Aaron and to us. He brought the best out of other people.

One afternoon, we were having a coffee and scone in a café, and a waitress got talking to us about Aaron. When we went to settle the bill, we were told that the staff had had a whip-round and there was nothing for us to pay. We appreciated such kindness and generosity; the only downside was that we felt unable to go in that cafe again, lest they thought we were after another 'freebie'.

One Sunday, a pastor was staying with us for the day and he wanted to know about Aaron. As we related to him what had happened, tears were flowing down his cheeks. That day, I saw a side to that man I had never seen before.

When Andrew got married in 2007, we were moved when he chose Aaron to be his best man. This was something we had never anticipated, but Andrew said, "Aaron is my brother; he will be my best man." On the day itself, Aaron had three assistants – one to hold the rings, one to sign the register and one to make the speech – but Aaron was the official best man.

The only people Aaron did not bring the best out of were the government. He received through the post a 'Return to Work Questionnaire' and when I telephoned the relevant government department, I got no joy – the form must be completed. It became a bit of a joke, and when the phone rang I would say to Pat, "Perhaps another job interview for Aaron!"

Aaron brought the best out in people except, with some, not where their attitude to God was concerned. Amongst the many who nursed and cared for Aaron there were believers, but there were also some who were atheists. They were professional and never openly advertised their atheism to us, but we heard it from other sources. Seeing the suffering of children was the only excuse they needed for rejecting any notion of a caring, loving God.

How true it is that 'the same sun which melts the wax also hardens the clay'. Distressing circumstances draw some people to God in repentance and faith, whilst others harden their hearts and continue in their unbelief. For Christians, suffering is a mystery but the cause lies not with God but in Genesis chapter 3, with man. How wonderful to know that one day there will be a new heaven and a new earth – a day when paradise will be restored (Revelation 21:1-4).

Aaron could do nothing for himself; he was entirely dependent on other people for all his needs to be met. This was a daily reminder to Pat and me of our utter dependence upon God. It is so easy to act as though we are independent beings but it is "in him we live and move and have our being" (Acts 17:28). We are dependent upon Him for the food we eat, the air we breathe, even for the very beat of our pulse. If this is true in the physical realm, it is just as true in the spiritual. "Salvation comes from the Lord" (Jonah 2:9). We cannot contribute anything; it is all down to His grace and His mercy.

As we fostered Aaron, Pat and I were occasionally saddened by the attitude of some believers. The implication was that it would be far better for him if the Lord was to take him and that we should not seek any medical intervention to prolong his life. Every human being is made in the image of God and therefore not only do they have a dignity but they have a purpose in the plan of God. This – more than we could initially ever have imagined – was to be true of Aaron.

As a pastor with a wife and two young children, money was sometimes tight and unexpected expenses proved to be a challenge. One morning, the car needed a new tyre, and as Pat and I sat in the waiting room at Kwik Fit, the mechanic came with the news that we needed not just one tyre but four. Our hearts sank, as we knew that once the tyres had been paid for, we would have nothing in reserve. As we travelled back to Ingleton, Pat said there was no alternative – she would have to find a job. This was something we had never anticipated, as the children were young and Pat wanted to be available to work within the church. It seemed, however, to be a case of 'needs must'.

We had lunch, and that very afternoon we had a phone call from Social Services. They were asking us to consider taking Aaron as a foster child. This we did, and as a result of the fostering allowances we received, there was no need for Pat to find work outside of the home. With such a provision from the Lord, how could we doubt that God had a plan and a purpose for Aaron?

During my time in the pastorate, again and again Pat and I came to see what an asset he was in the work. I have joked that when Aaron left school, he became Assistant Pastor of Ingleton Evangelical Church, and though a joke, it contains more than a measure of truth. Aaron was an icebreaker and people who might not have been sympathetic to the Gospel I preached were often more sympathetic to us because of Aaron.

Through Aaron we had opportunities to share the Gospel that otherwise we might not have had. We had invitations to speak at men's meetings, ladies' meetings, coffee mornings, church lunches and young people's meetings. With young people we emphasised that Aaron's disabilities were the result of drug-taking and we hoped that the sight of a severely handicapped young man might act as a deterrent to some, tempted to experiment with such lethal substances.

With Aaron we proved the truth of Paul's words to the Corinthians: "But God chose the foolish things of the world to shame the wise; God chose the weak things of the world to shame the strong. God chose the lowly things of this world and the despised things – and the things that are not – to nullify the things that are, so that no one may boast before him" (1 Corinthians 1:27-29).

When we were on holiday in Derbyshire a number of years ago, an elderly Christian lady made an interesting comment. "How wonderful it is," she said, "that Aaron has never knowingly sinned." I could never say that of myself but it was true of Aaron. Nevertheless, Aaron was still a sinner because we all inherit a sinful nature from Adam. It is, however, my conviction that babies and those without the mental capacity to understand the Gospel, through the grace of God, are covered by the sacrifice of Christ.

King David's baby died when he was just seven days old and David made the poignant statement, "I will go to him, but he will not return to me" (2 Samuel 12:23). David was to be "in the house of the Lord for ever" (Psalm 23:6) and he confidently affirms that his child is already there. We share the confidence of King David that the soul of Aaron is now 'safe in the arms of Jesus'.

What about his body? Paul speaks about "the redemption of our bodies" (Romans 8:23) and states with certainty that the Lord Jesus Christ "will transform our lowly bodies so that they will be like his glorious body" (Philippians 3:21). With respect and with sorrow we placed Aaron's body in the grave at Ingleton Cemetery, but that is only his temporary resting place. When Christ returns, the 'dead in Christ' will rise and Aaron then will be the possessor of a resurrected body – a perfect body fitted for the new heaven and the new earth. This is a prospect that thrills our hearts. In that day Aaron will speak, he will run, he will do all the things that he could never do on earth. The paediatrician was wrong when she said that "Aaron will never be able to thank you"; in the new heaven and the new earth he will.

Life without Aaron will never be quite the same and we are having to adjust to a new situation. My regular Saturday night routine was to give Aaron a jacuzzi and then together we watched Dad's Army. Though one of my favourite television programmes, for several months afterwards I was not able to watch it, as the association was too painful. This is all part of the grieving process and the price we pay for having loved someone.

Paul says we "do not grieve like the rest of mankind, who have no hope" (1 Thessalonians 4:13) and whilst there are days when our grief is greater than our hope, we thank the Lord for those days when our hope is so much greater than our grief. We thank God that the baby who initially only came for one year 'got his feet under the table' and stayed for over twenty-eight years.

We are grateful for all the time we spent with Aaron on earth and we look forward to that day when we shall meet him again in heaven. These sentiments are movingly expressed in a poem written by a cousin of Pat and received shortly after Aaron's death:

> *Don't weep too long – remember I'm with Jesus*
> *Don't grieve too long – because I went away*
> *Life has its changes and its disappointments*
> *I know you're sad because I couldn't stay.*
>
> *We've shared so much – I've looked and laughed and even*
> *Expressed so much – through limitations too,*
> *But from the best of all we shared together*
> *I treasured most – that I was loved by you.*
> *Don't weep too long – dear heart – the battle's over*
> *The days of life's uncertainties are passed*
> *The muddled, earthbound, slowing of the senses,*
> *My failing days – I've left them all at last.*
>
> *But here, beneath a sky of shining splendour*
> *Where scented blossoms spread the grassy lea*
> *The Lord and I – we sing the songs of Zion.*
> *There's nowhere else that I would rather be.*
>
> *But longing must resign itself to waiting*
> *God only knows how long we'll be apart*
> *So, when my Jesus tells me that you're coming*
> *I'll rise and run to welcome you, dear heart.*
>
> *Don't grieve too long.*

Pearl Malloy

Contact the Author

To contact the author, please write to:

John Mollitt,
Westgate,
Croft Road,
Ingleton,
Carnforth,
Lancs.
LA6 3BZ

Or send an email to:

john.mollitt@btinternet.com

Also by the Author

How Shall They Hear?
ISBN 978-1-911086-43-7

This collection of memoirs paints the life of a country preacher in broad strokes, through poignant anecdotes that will at times make you smile, at other times pause to reflect.

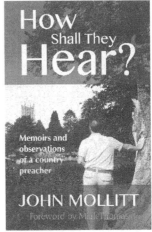

"John's reminiscing is both heart-warming and at times amusing. Preaching his first sermon to his brother at the age of ten, he later proclaimed the gospel widely in the open air, at children's missions, throughout a long serving pastorate and now in an itinerant ministry to rural fellowships. This has provided him not only with a score of anecdotes, but more significantly with a sympathetic understanding of the life of small village churches." – Brian H. Edwards

Truth in a Nutshell
ISBN 978-1-910197-76-9

This book of meditations contains over 100 scriptures and anecdotes. Taken from the life and experiences of itinerant preacher, John Mollitt, each story illustrates a key lesson from the scripture being studied. Organised by topic, these short pieces are perfect both for daily readings and as a resource for Bible teaching.

"This is a very personal and precious book, containing nuggets of pure gold. The material will be helpful to Christians, challenging to unbelievers, a real comfort and blessing to struggling Christians and a very helpful resource for preachers!" – Peter Parkinson, Co-founder, Caring for Life

Available from all good bookshops of from the publisher's webstore:

www.onwardsandupwardspublishing.com/brand/mollitt-john